Prime Time Plays

BASEBALL'S CRAZIEST CATCHES!

by Shawn Pryor

CAPSTONE PRESS
a capstone imprint

Capstone Captivate is published by Capstone Press, an imprint of Capstone.
1710 Roe Crest Drive, North Mankato, Minnesota 56003
www.capstonepub.com

SPORTS ILLUSTRATED KIDS is a trademark of ABG-SI LLC. Used with permission.

Library of Congress Cataloging-in-Publication Data
Names: Pryor, Shawn, author.
Title: Baseball's craziest catches! / by Shawn Pryor.
Description: North Mankato, Minnesota : Capstone Press, 2021. | Series: Sports illustrated kids prime time plays | Includes index. | Audience: Ages 8-11 | Audience: Grades 4-6 | Summary: "Crack! When the bat meets the ball, the gloves are up and it's prime time on the diamond. From sliding snags in the outfield to body-battering grabs at the wall, experience the craziest clutch catches from pro baseball's biggest superstars. These spectacular snatches will leave you spell-bound!"—Provided by publisher.
Identifiers: LCCN 2020025088 (print) | LCCN 2020025089 (ebook) | ISBN 9781496695840 (library binding) | ISBN 9781496696878 (paperback) | ISBN 9781977153845 (pdf)
Subjects: LCSH: Baseball—History—Juvenile literature. | Fielding (Baseball)—Juvenile literature.
Classification: LCC GV867.5 .P79 2021 (print) | LCC GV867.5 (ebook) | DDC 796.357—dc23
LC record available at https://lccn.loc.gov/2020025088
LC ebook record available at https://lccn.loc.gov/2020025089

Image Credits
AP Images: ASSOCIATED PRESS, 16, Elaine Thompson, 19, 26, Gary Stewart, 15, Jeff Roberson, 8, Matt Slocum, 21; Getty Images: Jonathan Daniel, 9, MediaNews Group/Boston Herald, 23, New York Daily News Archive, 13, bottom 25, The Washington Post, 7, top 11, bottom 11, Tim Warner, top 11, bottom 11; Newscom: Anthony J. Causi/Icon SMI, top 25, DAVID JOLES/KRT/, 29; Shutterstock: Beto Chagas, Cover, BK_graphic, design element throughout; Sports Illustrated: Al Tielemans, 18, Erick W. Rasco, 28, John Iacono, 5, 17, Robert Beck, 14

Editorial Credits
Editor: Christopher Harbo; Designer: Sarah Bennett; Media Researcher: Eric Gohl; Production Specialist: Katy LaVigne

All internet sites appearing in back matter were available and accurate when this book was sent to press.

TABLE OF CONTENTS

Words in **bold** are in the glossary.

INTRODUCTION

WHAT A CATCH!

It's the bottom of the ninth. With the bases loaded and two outs, the pitcher clings to a one-run lead. He winds up and fires a blazing fastball. CRACK! A long fly ball sails to straightaway center. The center fielder dashes back, back, back. . . . With a giant leap, he reaches up and snags the ball above the wall. What a catch! Game over!

What's more exciting than monster hits in Major League Baseball (MLB)? The head-spinning catches that take those hits away. From legendary leaps to modern-day magical moments, get ready for the big league grabs that stunned players and fans alike. These are baseball's craziest catches!

Fans look on as Melky
Cabrera of the New
York Yankees makes
a stunning catch over
the outfield wall.

CHAPTER 1

BIG PLAYS IN BIG MOMENTS

Nothing is more exciting than making a stunning catch when it matters most. Here are some of the best snatches that dazzled fans in recent playoff matchups.

Rendon's Super-Stretch Catch

Third baseman Anthony Rendon was a cornerstone of the 2019 Washington Nationals. His clutch hits and amazing catches launched the team into the playoffs. Naturally, in Game 3 of the National League Championship Series (NLCS), he was in the right place at the right time.

FACT

In middle school, Rendon played basketball and baseball and was also on the track team.

The moment came in the top of the third inning. St. Louis Cardinals batter Paul DeJong hit a blazing **line drive** in the gap between **shortstop** and third base. The shortstop was nowhere close enough to make a move on the ball. But Rendon, who stood a bit back at third, leaped to his left. Extended like a superhero in flight, he snatched the one-hopper from the air. Then he scrambled to his feet and threw to first to rob DeJong of an easy base hit.

Anthony Rendon dives to catch the hot one-hopper hit by Paul DeJong in Game 3 of the 2019 NLCS.

Taylor's Swift Slide

In the 2018 NLCS, Chris Taylor of the Los Angeles Dodgers proved speed is what you need. During Game 7 against the Milwaukee Brewers, he made one of the wildest catches in playoff history.

It was the bottom of the fifth inning. With a runner on base, the Brewers' best hitter, Christian Yelich, stepped to the plate. At the same time, Taylor moved closer to the foul line in left field. He thought Yelich would try to poke the ball down the line. Instead, Yelich drilled it into the center-field gap. To prevent a run from scoring, Taylor sprinted into the gap. With a leaping slide across the warning track, he made a nearly impossible over-the-shoulder catch! The remarkable grab didn't just keep the Brewers from scoring. It helped lift the Dodgers to the World Series.

Chris Taylor turns his back to the infield to track the high fly ball off of Christian Yelich's bat.

Cody Bellinger leaps to avoid a collision as Taylor makes the sliding over-the-shoulder catch on the warning track.

FACT

Taylor started the game at second base before moving to left field in the third inning.

Brantley's Brilliant Double Play

Houston Astros outfielder Michael Brantley wasn't always known for his **defense**. His manager would even pull him from games when a better outfielder was needed. But Brantley kept working on his skills. And his hard work paid off in Game 6 of the 2019 American League Championship Series (ALCS).

In the seventh inning, the New York Yankees' Aaron Hicks hit a **blooper** to shallow left field. It looked like Brantley wasn't going to catch it. As the short hit dropped toward the ground, Brantley raced in, dove, and scooped up the ball! Then he jumped up and fired it to first as base runner Aaron Judge scrambled back to the bag. **Double play**! The catch ended the Yankees' inning, and the Astros went on to win the game and head to the World Series.

Michael Brantley rushes in for a diving catch (top) and then throws to first base (right) to complete a double play in Game 6 of the 2019 ALCS.

CHAPTER 2

ALL-STAR CATCHES

Some players make catches that stick with fans for **generations**. Here are a few amazing grabs from baseball's best All-Stars.

The Catch

Willie Mays was one of the best players in baseball history. As an outfielder for the New York Giants, he made one of the greatest catches of all time. In fact, it was so great that it is simply known as "The Catch."

"The Catch" happened during Game 1 of the 1954 World Series against the Cleveland Indians. With the game tied in the eighth inning, Indians batter Vic Wertz hit a deep fly ball to center field. Because Mays was playing in shallow center, he had to turn and run to catch up with it. As the ball arced toward the warning track, Mays stuck out his glove and made an over-the-shoulder catch for the ages! His amazing grab kept the Indians from scoring. The Giants won the game in extra innings.

Willie Mays turns his back to the infield to make "The Catch" in Game 1 of the 1954 World Series.

The Spider-Man Catch

By 1991, 21-year-old Ken Griffey Jr. had already been a Gold Glove winner and a two-time All-Star. The center fielder for the Seattle Mariners was a great hitter. But he also had a gift for robbing **opposing** batters of home runs and extra-base hits.

One of Griffey's greatest catches came on May 25, 1991, against the Texas Rangers. When Rangers **slugger** Rubén Sierra smashed a pitch deep to right center field, Griffey took off. While keeping his eye on the ball, Griffey crossed the warning track and slammed against the outfield wall. Somehow, he still made the grab, robbing Sierra of an extra-base hit. After rolling on the ground, Griffey shook off the pain. The crowd went wild.

FACT

Gold Glove awards are given to the best fielding players at each position in both the American League and the National League during the regular season.

Ken Griffey Jr. crashes into the outfield wall but still holds onto the ball to rob Rangers slugger Rubén Sierra of an extra-base hit.

Bo Knows Great Catches

In the late 1980s, no one was quite like Bo Jackson. He played pro baseball and football and was famous for his strength and speed. As an outfielder for the Kansas City Royals, he made catches that sent fans into a frenzy.

Fans expecting a home run ball can't believe their eyes when Bo Jackson makes the catch instead.

One such catch came on July 10, 1988, against the New York Yankees. As Jackson covered left field, Yankees slugger Jack Clark launched a ball deep to left field. Jackson quickly **backpedaled**, following the ball all the way to the warning track. With perfect timing, he jumped and snatched the ball just as it soared beyond the wall. Fans in the stands shook their heads in awe as Jackson robbed Clark of a homer.

Yount Saves the Day

Some catches save games. Others make history. On April 14, 1987, Milwaukee Brewers star Robin Yount's leaping grab in center on the final out saved a **no-hitter** for pitcher Juan Nieves. It was the first no-hitter in Brewers history!

Yount began his pro baseball career as a shortstop before moving to the outfield in 1985.

CHAPTER 3

HOW DID THEY DO THAT?

Baseball's best catches look almost impossible to make. Here are some sweet snags that will have you asking, "How did they do that?"

Henderson Holds On

By 2000, Rickey Henderson had played in the big leagues for 22 years. But the 41-year-old showed no signs of slowing down. The speedy left fielder for the Seattle Mariners could still steal bases and make great running catches.

All-Time Gold Glove Winners

18 Greg Maddux, Pitcher
16 Jim Kaat, Pitcher
16 Brooks Robinson, Third Baseman
13 Ozzie Smith, Shortstop
13 Iván Rodríguez, Catcher
12 Roberto Clemente, Outfielder
12 Willie Mays, Outfielder
11 Omar Vizquel, Shortstop
11 Keith Hernandez, First Baseman

Greg Maddux

Henderson's speed was on full display in a game on August 1, 2000, against the Boston Red Sox. When Troy O'Leary hit a deep pop-up along the left-field line, Henderson gave chase. The ball was going toward foul territory—but that didn't stop him. Henderson raced to the sideline and fell backward into the stands as he made the catch for the out!

Rickey Henderson goes beyond the boundaries of the field as he tips backward into the stands to catch the foul ball for an out.

Matthews' Stunning Spinner

Outfielder Gary Matthews Jr. had a great season for the Texas Rangers in 2006. He hit the most home runs of his **career** and played in the All-Star Game. He also made some truly breathtaking catches in the outfield.

One of his most stunning grabs came in a July 1 game against the Houston Astros. When the Astros' Mike Lamb hit a towering shot to deep center field, it looked like an easy home run. But out of nowhere, Matthews raced toward the outfield wall. At the last second, he leaped and did a 360-degree spin. With his arm stretched completely over the wall, he nabbed the ball. Lamb's sure-thing home run turned into a surefire out!

Swan-Dive Slide

In 2018, Cody Bellinger made one of the most graceful catches in recent playoff history. His diving, sliding catch in the tenth inning of Game 4 of the NLCS helped the Los Angeles Dodgers beat the Milwaukee Brewers with style.

Gary Matthews Jr. reaches high over the outfield wall to take a home run away from Astros slugger Mike Lamb.

Benintendi's Impossible Grab

Boston Red Sox outfielder Andrew Benintendi's catch in Game 4 of the 2018 ALCS should never have happened. Even the MLB's **statistics** tool, Statcast, **calculated** Benintendi's chances of making the grab at only 21 percent. But he beat the odds in a big way!

In the bottom of the ninth, Boston clung to a two-run lead. With the bases loaded, one of the Astros' best hitters, Alex Bregman, slapped a blooper to left field. The short hit should have scored enough runs for the Astros to win. But Benintendi did the impossible. He rushed in, stretched out, and slipped his glove between the ball and the turf. His sliding snag won the game for the Red Sox!

FACT

Benintendi's catch was named the Associated Press' Play of the Year for 2018.

Andrew Benintendi slips his glove beneath the ball just in time to turn a bloop hit into a game-ending out.

CHAPTER 4

UNBELIEVABLE!

While some catches look impossible, others are downright unbelievable. Here are just a few remarkable catches that will make your jaw drop!

The Dive

Derek Jeter was a legendary shortstop for the New York Yankees. During 20 seasons, he was a **Rookie** of the Year, a 14-time All-Star, a five-time Gold Glove winner, and a five-time Silver Slugger. He always found ways to make great plays—especially against the Boston Red Sox.

In a July 1, 2004, matchup with the Red Sox, Jeter even put his body on the line to make a catch. On a pop-up down the third-base line, the shortstop took off running across the field. Jeter had the speed to catch up with the ball, but he couldn't stop his **momentum**. Three steps after making the grab, he landed headfirst in the stands. Forever known as "The Dive," the catch earned Jeter a battered face and a ton of love from his fans.

Derek Jeter flies into the stands after making a stunning catch (top) and then walks back to the dugout with the battle wounds to show for his extra effort (right).

The Birthday Gift

Mike Trout is one of the most popular players in Los Angeles Angels history. As their center fielder, he makes a lot of prime time plays. But few have been bigger than the one he made on his twenty-fifth birthday.

On August 7, 2016, the Angels squared off against the Seattle Mariners. Tied in the bottom of the fourth, the Mariners had the bases loaded with no outs. That's when Leonys Martín smashed a deep shot to center field. Trout scrambled back, leaped, and caught the ball before it dipped behind the wall. After falling to the ground, he scrambled to his feet and threw the ball back to the infield. One run scored, but Trout's birthday gift had robbed the Mariners of a grand slam!

Mike Trout reaches up to make a grand-slam-stealing snag that proves to be the icing on his twenty-fifth birthday cake.

Hunting It Down

During his 19-year career, Torii Hunter was one of the best center fielders in baseball. He was known for his power, speed, and mastery in the outfield. For proof, just look to the 2002 All-Star Game.

In the first inning of the game, Hunter waited in center field as Barry Bonds loomed over the plate. Bonds was known for blasting towering home runs. Pitchers feared him—and for good reason. With a massive cut, Bonds sent the ball soaring to deep right center field. It was definitely going out of the park—or was it? Hunter raced to the wall and jumped as high as he could. Sticking his glove up, the Minnesota Twin robbed one of the greatest home-run hitters of all time!

FACT

On September 25, 2015, outfielder Mookie Betts almost toppled over the center-field wall! Why? To rob Chris Davis of a home run and to end the game!

Torii Hunter leaps and stretches for a towering shot to take away an almost certain home run from Barry Bonds during the 2002 All-Star Game.

GLOSSARY

backpedal (BAK-ped-uhl)—to move backward quickly

blooper (BLOOP-ur)—a weak hit that flies just beyond the reach of the infielders in baseball

calculate (KAL-kyuh-layt)—to find a solution by using math

career (kuh-REER)—the time spent by a person while doing a particular profession

defense (di-FENSS)—the act of stopping points from being scored in a game

double play (DUH-buhl PLAY)—two outs on the same play

generation (jen-uh-RAY-shuhn)—a group of people born around the same time

line drive (LINE DRIVE)—a batted ball that is hit hard in the air in a straight line

momentum (moh-MEN-tuhm)—the forward motion gained by the development of events

no-hitter (no-HIT-ur)—a game in which one team doesn't allow the other team to get a hit

opposing (uh-POZE-ing)—on the opposite side

rookie (RUK-ee)—a first-year player

shortstop (SHORT-stop)—in baseball, the defensive position between second and third base

slugger (SLUG-uhr)—a batter who gets a lot of hits

statistics (stuh-TISS-tiks)—the science of collecting numerical facts, such as a player's achievements on the field

READ MORE

Braun, Eric. *Pro Baseball's Underdogs: Players and Teams Who Shocked the Baseball World.* North Mankato, MN: Capstone Press, 2018.

Doeden, Matt. *G.O.A.T. Baseball Teams.* Minneapolis: Lerner Publishing Group, 2021.

Weakland, Mark. *Baseball Records.* Mankato, MN: Black Rabbit Books, 2021.

INTERNET SITES

Little League
www.littleleague.org

Major League Baseball
www.mlb.com

Sports Illustrated Kids
www.sikids.com

INDEX